How to create your most successful year ever

Even during a year of crisis

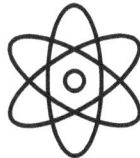

WORKBOOK PRESS LLC
187 E Warm Springs Rd,
Suite B285 Las Vegas NV 89119 USA

Website: https://workbookpress.com/
Hotline: 1-888-818-4856
Email: admin@workbookpress.com

Ordering Information:

Quantity sales. Special discounts are available on quantity purchases by corporations, associations, and others. For details, contact the publisher at the address above.

Library of Congress Control Number:

ISBN-13:   978-1-961845-20-6   Paperback Version
               978-1-961845-21-3   Digital Version

REV. DATE: 12/20/2024

Medical disclaimer

This book does not offer medical or professional advice. The ideas presented are not pertinent to psychological conditions or disorders that require medical treatment.

With ongoing depression or mental health issues, please consult a medical professional. If you are experiencing suicidal thoughts phone a suicide crisis hotline in your country. Search online or visit: -www.iasp.info

CONTENTS

For creative women

everywhere.

The world needs you

Are you ready to step up?

You are a

one-of-a-kind-unique

YOUR NAME

TODAY'S DATE

Section One

MESSAGE FROM GWYNETH

I am an Author, Motivational Speaker, Creative Business Consultant, Producer, and Host of Afrikaba Radio, as well as the CEO of the Afrikaba Festival, which was founded with the goal of highlighting the rich diversity of culture and talent from Africa and diasporan descendants across the globe.

My professional career includes information technology, the creative industries in film, television, radio, music, and the healing arts. I have started entrepreneurial ventures, formed partnerships, and managed projects for renowned corporations such as the BBC, Financial Times, and the UK Fire & Rescue Service, among others. As a consultant, I had the privilege of mentoring creative business owners and artists across all genres. I have worked with people from all walks of life, spanning many cultures giving me a deep understanding of the obstacles faced by individuals trying to get an idea off the ground.

Are you aware of your unique abilities, and how to use them in creating greater possibilities for your life and living?

With a passion for creativity and a commitment to uplifting others, my work provides a bridge between creativity, business, and the healing arts. I strive to inspire and support individuals in realizing their dreams and uncovering their fullest potential, and especially love helping women discover their true strengths.

We are more than titles. Your life is a journey of discovery. The challenge is to unearth the hidden gems within the depth of your experiences.

Each one of us holds a unique position in the grand tapestry of life. Our voices, actions, and decisions weave the fabric of our shared existence on this earth. You do not need permission to shine.

YOU play a relevant part in shaping the world by being here, bringing the best of yourself to your daily interactions and being authentically YOU.

Do not underestimate the power of one individual choosing to step out and do something new. History is filled with examples of solitary figures whose courage to break free from limitations has led to profound transformations. Whether it is a scientist pioneering groundbreaking research, an artist challenging conventional aesthetics, or an activist standing against injustice, the choices of a single person can spark movements, inspire change, and alter the course of history.

All knowledge comes from life. Fortunately, you do not have to live through every experience yourself to gain insight and gather wisdom because you can learn from others. When we share our philosophies, we learn from each other finding new ways to navigate through life.

We all face challenges that may not feel good at the time yet present an opportunity to grow.

Embracing these challenges with a willingness to learn can transform obstacles into stepping-stones to success.

Because your influence extends beyond your personal achievements. You can shape the world negatively or influence it positively. Your intentions, decisions and actions touch the lives of others, even people you do not know.

I drafted this book first for me, then designed it to assist other women in breaking through self-limiting barriers to success. Allow my passion and motivation help you in bringing your greatest ideas to life. Jump in and make this your best year ever!

Gwyneth

Are you choosing to live a

one-size-fits-all life?

INTRODUCTION

This book is part philosophical review, and part journal. It is a personal development tool that works from the inside out to get you ready for even greater success.

Success is often acquainted with money and assets that generate wealth, however, some people's thinking about riches and use of money merely creates stress and misery.

The means to generate income is important in the modern world as it allows you to provide food, clothes, and shelter for yourself and your family. It grants you the ability to contribute financially to others and to progress your own dreams, but without a strong emotional foundation, money alone cannot bring you joy.

One of the cornerstones of true success is personal growth. This involves continuous learning and self-development.

A successful person is someone who strives to reach their full potential, whether through education, skill development, or creative endeavors. Part of personal growth is in navigating relationships, health, and contribution to society.

The journey to success is not filled with high fives and hoorahs. There will be tears, frustration and discomfort but if you persevere you will find fulfillment from setting your goals, overcoming the obstacles that stood in your way, to then experience the joy of your personal achievements.

At the end of the day, success is a life well lived. It may not be a life of complete comfort but one where you find harmony within yourself that you then share with others.

Use this book to support you in making changes that free you from feelings of inadequacy. Let it remind you of how unique you truly be.

The information in this book is not offered as medical or professional advice. What it contains is knowledge and experience gathered from life. It is full of questions, each one designed to heighten your awareness and root out the restrictions you impose on yourself. Some questions are repeated throughout the book.

Looking at your life with an open and curious mind gives you an opportunity to start removing self-imposed restrictions and their effects on your life.

This book was not designed to be kept on a shelf, and neither are you.

you are meant to shine in your own unique way, and this book was created to help you do that. It is designed to be used, handled, pages folded back, and carried in a bag. It contains questions, empty spaces, and blank pages for your reflections.

The words you write here are precious so when you see an empty space, write on it, and even make notes in the margins. The beauty of writing on paper is that it slows things down. It gives you time to process ideas, and it leaves you with something tangible to reflect on later.

If you would like additional writing pages, see page 311 for other journals created as part of this series.

You will see the following icon throughout the book as a reminder to write something in the spaces provided.

Let the questions help you dream and catalyze your next big success.

By taking action on your ideas and following your dreams, you become a beacon for others. This increases the richness and depth of what life offers you in return.

Are you ready?

What is your motivation for change at this time? (Make a note below)

How do you hope to feel by the time you finish this journal?

The world needs YOU Are you ready to step up?

WHAT YOU'LL LEARN

This book will guide you towards deepening awareness of your unique abilities, and encourage you to take bigger, bolder steps. It will direct you to remember the following:

- That your abilities are an asset
- That you have the potential to create beyond your limitations
- That it is time to get energized and motivated
- To recognize the voices within that put you down, and make them work for you, rather than against you
- To remind you to bring your ideas from thought into everyday reality

Give yourself the opportunity to learn something new. If an idea challenges your beliefs, do not reject it outright. Sit with it for a while. Ask the question "what about this, do I not understand?". You do not have to accept an idea as right for you but gaining a clearer picture of it may help you understand someone else's point of view.

Sometimes information comes to us when we are emotionally not ready, and it is not until years later that we really get it.

The words *'need to'*, *'should'* or *'must'* in this book are used for expediency, The only thing you *'need to do'* is to keep breathing so substitute the words *'should'* or *'must'* with *'I could'* or *'I choose to'*.

Allocate time to be with yourself, be patient with the process but do not wait to begin. You only have a limited number of days in your life. Do not waste them!

Are you ready to release, delete and un-create what does not work for you? Grab a pen or pencil and make a start.

What changes are you trying to implement in your life?

What three things can you do today to start implementing those changes?

MAKE A START

Be aware that the higher you fly, and the greater your success, the more likely that you may be misunderstood, misquoted, denigrated, and misjudged by those who are jealous of you.

Friends whose ambition surpass your friendship may want to capitalize on your success. You will encounter challenging people and have to manage demanding situations. Do not let that stop you or stand in your way.

Learning to trust yourself, your emotions, and your abilities, will help you manage your most successful, and sometimes most confounding of times.

Learn from your failures and let your difficulties teach you new strategies. Use uncertainty to sharpen your skills. As you consistently pay attention to your personal development you will surpass even your own expectations. Each win will spur you on to greater success.

Ask questions and look inwards at the patterns in your life that contribute to your personal dilemmas.

You are stronger when you know your 'why', more likely to follow the voice urging you to reach for your dreams, and more willing to do whatever it takes to accomplish it. when you have a compelling reason for the disruption caused to your life. Are you motivated to make a better life for your children? Are you going through divorce, menopause, empty-nest, or a health crisis? Do you feel called to advocate for a cause?

You may not think that you are ready, but circumstances may have already forced change upon you.

Get ready to create your life as a masterpiece of beauty, abundance, confidence, and joy,

Are you hesitating?

Let go… Jump in.

Take five minutes to think about your reasons for picking up this book then make a note of them in the space below.

Start with Inspiration but

remember that Motivation

follows Action

SUMMARIZE THE LAST 12 MONTHS

What has taken place in your life over the last 12 months?

WHAT IS YOUR MEASURE OF SUCCESS

Today's Date_____

How will you know that you have achieved your goals? How will you know that you have achieved the success you hoped for?

Make a note below of what you will be doing, how much money you will be generating, and where you will be living.

What challenges do you expect to
meet in stretching for your goals?

What can you do to overcome those challenges?

SELF REFLECTION

What new skills do you now have
and what new awareness have you
received?

Is it time now to bring the

next greatest version of

You to life?

34

Section Two

DISCOVER YOUR MAGNIFICENCE

There are billions of people on earth, yet there is no other person, and never has there been anyone, with the combination of experiences, skill, and innate talent, which is you but since human eyes look out at the world and not into the body, we have a tendency to observe and judge other people. It takes some persuasion to turn our gaze inward to reflect on ourselves. Are you ready to evolve?

Is it time you elevated your life and gave it the push it deserves?

This section begins your journey to opening your mind to change. It will reflect on personal responsibility, your power to choose, and then decide the influences on your life going forward.

Go unveil your magnificence!

What would you like your life to look like in 5 years?

Continue to look ahead to the next five years. Keep refining your goals, whilst allowing your dream to evolve.

If you were to take a single step towards achieving your dream, what could that be?

KNOW YOUR LIMITS

Our interests and inclinations lead us to pay attention to certain activities and leave others behind. Each of us is better at some things and not so great at other activities. We all have limitations, but do not have to be defined by them.

You do not have to be limited by what you cannot do because you have the ability to learn new skills.

On the other hand, just because you can do something does not mean that you should be the one to do it.

Consider the following questions:-

- What is your time worth, and is it worth your time to learn that skill?
- Might your time be best used doing something else?
- Would you be better off paying for it?

What new skills do you need to learn
to help you realize your dreams?

What do you recognize and
acknowledge as limitations or tasks that
you do not like to do?

What do you need help with?

FREE YOUR MIND

We fight for autonomy and self-determination. Even children too young to know the meaning of the words, wrestle to have their own way.

Freedom is an idea. It is an ideal that does not come free, and may not fully exist, yet people advocated for, fought for, and died for the civil liberties, and freedom of choice that many of us enjoy today.

We follow rules because it makes life easier for the majority. If we break the rules there are consequences and we lose certain freedoms. This does not just happen in other countries it happens in yours too. In fact, all societies restrict personal freedoms in one way or another.

Despite the freedom afforded you, from the moment you were born you were indoctrinated into beliefs about yourself, about other people, and entrained in ways of thinking, and patterns of behavior so that you can conform and fit into society.

In repressive regimes it takes courage to claim the freedom and rights that some of us take for granted.

In most countries across the globe, what has been described as gender apartheid exists, where women have less freedom than men, earn less than men, and granted fewer opportunities.

Women in some cultures are refused education, sold into domestic and sexual slavery, their voices and freedom of expression silenced, and some live in constant risk of rape and murder. Women in any country can be subjected to violent criminal acts, often at the hands of people they know.

What will you do with your freedom? How will you express yourself in honor of women who do not share your rights?

No matter where you live, the most significant choice you can make, is to be the mistress of your mind because an independent mind has more freedom than most and not as easily controlled.

Freedom does not mean anarchy. Responsibility, maturity, and leadership are interconnected with mental freedom. No one can free your mind but you. Other people become catalysts for your change, they can encourage, support, and cheer you on, but nobody can give you freedom of thought.

To become mistress of your mind start by becoming aware of the habitual thoughts that try to hijack your confidence, which try to deny your strengths and uses fear in an attempt to limit your connection to others.

The negative ideas you entertain about yourself impair your ability to elevate your life and succeed at higher levels because when negative self-talk lives inside a person's psyche it can negatively reshape their personality, making them angry and hostile.

SHOW UP WITH INTENTION

In every moment, you are faced with a choice: how will you show up?

This question may seem simple yet holds profound significance in shaping your life and the world around you.

Choosing how you show up in the world is about being intentional with your appearance, your actions, and your mindset. It is about taking control of first impressions and acknowledging the impact you leave behind.

This idea is rooted in self-awareness. By understanding your values, strengths, and areas of growth, you can begin to align your actions with your inner calling. It requires a commitment to personal development and a willingness to reflect on your experiences in order to gain clarity on what matters most to you and how you can contribute meaningfully to the world.

Remember that you represent something, or someone so create your own rules for how you conduct yourself in any given situation, set standards for how you treat other people, for how you dress, for how you resolve conflict, for the type of language you use day to day.

Consider ahead of time how you will manage and maintain your composure when you are stressed. You may not get it right every single time but the more intention and effort you put in, the better you will get at remaining calm and composed.

Develop rituals and routines to help you maintain focus and discipline. Think about how you would like to show up in the world then answer the following questions.

If first impressions matter, describe how you would like to show up with your clothing and general appearance

If your environment can help or hinder your creativity, what type of environment would you like to live in and where?

In what ways would you express your creativity?

What qualities would you like to inspire both in yourself and in others?

RESPONSIBILITY & ACCOUNTABILITY

Adults carry responsibilities. If you do not have any responsibilities, then you are not fully living because first and foremost, you have a responsibility to create your own life.

Responsibility gives one a reason to get out of bed in the morning, to make better choices and to put meaningful action behind your words.

Here are some ideas to help keep you on track:-

- Do not allow yourself to aimlessly coast through life for prolonged periods of time

- Do not allow yourself to get sloppy in your work

- Do not make excuses for what you have or have not done

- Do not blame someone else for your shortcomings, learn from them.

Make yourself accountable for managing your time.

- Do what you say you will do

- Be prepared

- Turn up each day to represent yourself and do the work that life asks of you

Be responsible

- Accept responsibility for your outcomes

- Learn from your mistakes

- Make yourself accountable, especially to yourself

On the following page list the people in your life that you are responsible for and those to whom you are accountable.

Who are you responsible for...

Who are you accountable to...

HEALTH & HEALING

Without good health, everything else that you are trying to achieve loses its appeal. Physical, mental, and emotional well-being are essential components of a successful life. Maintaining a healthy lifestyle through exercise, proper nutrition, and stress management can help to ensure that you have the energy and vitality to pursue your dreams.

In the West we live in a state of low-level anxiety, which keeps the body in flight or fight mode. Over the long term this can result in chronic illness.

If you have difficulty finding answers to long-standing health issues, first seek medical advice to find out what might be going on. Choose professionals who can look at the underlying cause of your symptoms and offer solutions that steer your body towards health in a manner that respects you and your beliefs.

Claim responsibility for your healing journey

The physical body is just one aspect of being human, but we focus on it the most because it is what we see and touch, but healing happens on many levels.

Our bodies vibrate with energy that provides life and maintains health. Energy centers situated along pathways throughout the body collect and distribute energy in order to maintain vibrancy and health. These energy centers are called chakras and the pathways, meridians.

Each country has a healing tradition and name for the vibrational energy just discussed. In China the energy is called Chi and the practice Chinese Traditional

Medicine, Chi is the life force in every living thing. In India, the energy is called Prana and the practice known as Ayurvedic medicine. Other countries may have different names.

Western Medicine works on the physical body with surgery and medication to effect change. It can more speedily remove or change conditions that push the body into an adverse state but can also carry extreme side effects.

Holistic therapies work with Chi to remind your mind and body of the ability to heal. Acupuncture for example, uses fine needles to alter and rebalance the flow of Chi throughout the body in order to bring about health.

Herbs and homeopathy have lower side effects but work much slower to nudge your body towards health.

Bodywork such as yoga, massage, Access Bars, cranial-sacral therapy, and other modalities work to give you flexibility of body and mind. Psychotherapy, counselling, mentoring, and coaching may help you to overcome your lack of confidence.

Unless you have good medical reasons to do so, you do not have to limit your health choices. You can mix and match healing modalities until you find the combination that works for you.

People act as catalysts for your change, but you and your own body, bring about your healing.

To re-balance your emotions during stressful times, consider simple, easily accessible vibrational remedies that can often be bought over the counter from a pharmacy or health-store. These include flower essences, essential oils, herbs and adaptogens, for example Ashwagandha for stress, anxiety, and mood support.

When you are anxious, gently stroke your wrists and arms. This will help to calm your nervous system.

Access Bars are thirty-two points on the head that, when touched, effortlessly release thoughts, ideas, beliefs, emotions, and considerations that limit success. See: createayearofsuccess.com/other-resources for more information.

Another technique is Tapping. Also known as Emotional Freedom Technique (EFT) it uses acupressure points on the face, hands, and torso, along with specific phrases to help calm the nervous system. A search online will bring up more information.

The following list shows some highly effective natural tonics but be aware that they can affect your medications by ether increasing or decreasing medicinal effects:

- Ginseng

- Garlic

- Ginger

- Echinacea

- St John's Wort

- Ginkgo Biloba

- Black Cohosh

- Goldenseal

- Grapefruit.

Consult your pharmacist or your doctor about contraindications.

Your emotions, your state of mind, your environment, your DNA, the levels of you that you cannot see work together with the therapeutic modalities you choose, to bring about healing.

Whether you choose western medicine and Ayurvedic, or homeopathic and naturopathy, whatever your preference, remember that each healing modality has both strengths and weaknesses.

Do your research to find what works best for you. And make a note of the therapies you would like to try.

The table on the following page offers strategies that will assist you in maintaining optimal health.

Strategies for great health
• Hydrate with good clean water
• Nourish your body with quality food
• Do not sit all day
• Ensure that you move your body every day, several times a day
• Stretch, walk, be aware of breathing
• Get outside into the fresh air
• Minimize your stress and find the time to relax. Just make it happen
• Engage socially with other people
• Look for reasons to live and for what makes life feel worthwhile
• Actively support a cause or activity
• Schedule opportunities for fun

Strategies for great health
• Stay on the look-out for new, interesting, and enjoyable activities
• Find and engage your creativity
• Do not just entertain your mind, educate it
• Surround yourself with people who build a network of support
• Demonstrate what love is, and be willing to receive it
• Look for opportunities to smile
• Challenge yourself to grow by doing what seems difficult

IT STARTS WITH CHOICE

To live a successful life over the long term, be willing to change. Learn how to adapt, then allow yourself to grow into a newer version of you. The self you have not yet met. We are never too old to try something new.

How often have you stopped yourself from taking on a challenge because you secretly did not feel worthy enough?

Every step you take starts with a choice. A conscious decision to get from point A to point B. Are you making choices that will lead you to success or are you sleepwalking through life?

You can take charge of your life or live by default, If you allow others to choose for you, your life is not your own. You are living someone else's ideals. Other people may think they know better than you how to live your life, but you have the freedom to choose it.

If you find it difficult to take responsibility and make hard choices, take small steps. Choose what creates the greatest possibilities and generates the most joy and expansiveness in your life.

Train your body, educate your mind, give yourself a goal, and reprogram yourself for a more fulfilling life.

Your decisions do not have to be made as a 'Once and Done, they do not have to be forever. Add time limits that give you the freedom to change your mind. Try it in your mind first. If the idea is not a good fit, make a different choice.

This is not an excuse to be irresponsible, undependable, rash, or immature. It is an exercise to help you in making decisions that support your growth, your wellbeing, and your life.

Growing up I heard the following phrase over and over again... *"You made your bed hard, now you have to lie in it"*

The Jamaican dialect carries so much more emphasis, and it was a Jamaican who spoke those words, so it went more like...

"If yu mek yu bed hard, yu haffi lie in it!"

No doubt there is a historical reference to that phrase, but why would anyone want to lay in a hard, uncomfortable bed they do not like, and lay in it forever?

You have the right to change your mind and freedom to choose something different. Claim that right, own it and learn when and how to say "No, that doesn't work for me!"

You do not have to remain in an unhappy relationship, you do not have to stay in an unpleasant job.

YOU can chart your own course. YOU can generate 'joy' in your life by making decisions and taking steps that lead there.

To gain something important, you have to be willing to give up what stands in the way.

What do you need to give up in order to live the life that you would choose to live if you thought you could?

FEELING THE BLUES

Emotions are a biological response to a trigger, which we then interpret into a feeling. This is part of the human experience.

We all have periods of joy but also of sadness. If you wake up every day feeling as though a dark cloud sits over your head, this is a sign of depression. Ask for help.

If you find your circumstances, whether at home or work, unbearable, speak with somebody. Find help to understand the cause and begin envisioning a different future.

Do not let anyone convince you that things cannot change. Give yourself a clear objective and set goals that support a brighter future. Dig deep and find the energy to take action.

In order to survive, we learn to adapt to new situations. Unfortunately, that means we can also tune out or put up with what we should not be 'putting up with'.

When you feel low, get out of your head. Do something that takes your mind off what you are feeling and channel it into something creative. Motivate a friend by cheering them on or reach out to help cheer them up.

Thoughts possess a magnetic quality, like-attracting-like.

Change your state of mind by moving your body. Dance, sing, cook, sew, listen to music, make something, or visit a friend. Even watching a good movie can distract you from the low energetic state that you are in.

Keeping a journal is an effective way to monitor your happiness. It will show you what you might be ignoring and in fact, might be right in front of your face.

Joy, happiness, fun, and laughter are essential to a fulfilled life.

Depression attracts depression,
Laughter attracts laughter, and
Misery loves company.

If you were raised in a home with a depressive parent, there is a stronger likelihood that you too will experience depression. Make yourself available, and be proactive in creating the experience of joy, fun, and laughter.

Depression is the most common mental health illness in the world. It affects millions of people worldwide, especially women. It should not be minimized. Pay attention to your mind, Search online for Deepak Chopra and mindfulness training. [1]

---

[1] Important note:

This book does not offer medical or professional advice. With bipolar, schizophrenia, clinical depression or other ongoing mental health issues, please consult a medical professional.

If you experience suicidal thoughts, please find help and support. Consult a medical professional or contact a suicide crisis hotline. See www.iasp.info/suicidalthoughts.1.

What activities do you most enjoy?

What can you do to incorporate the
activities that you enjoy into your life?

What would you like your life to look like five years from now?

Do not copy what you wrote previously. Keep refreshing your ideas

SELF REFLECTION

What new skills do you now have
and what new awareness have you
received?

What would you like your life to look like five years from now?

Do not copy what you wrote previously. Keep refreshing your ideas

SELF REFLECTION

What new skills do you now have
and what new awareness have you
received?

Section Two - Self reflection

Continuously thinking
about your past keeps you
reliving the hurt of the past

Section Three

IS YOUR TIME NOW?

What you did or did not accomplish in the past is gone but you can learn from past mistakes to improve what you do now. There are countless reasons why you did not finish what you started, or did not start at all. Let the past take care of itself.

This section encourages you to open your mind to new possibilities, and to make a bigger commitment to exploring and sharing your abilities.

Is it time now for you to create a larger life?

If so, create a bigger vision.

If you are looking for an easy life, without challenge, you will not have a more expansive, accomplished life.

Challenges shape your character and help show what you are capable of achieving. They also teach you about the skills needed to fulfill your goals.

To enjoy a bigger life, you must be bold, and you must take action.

Is now the time for you to shine your light out into the world?

Answer the following 'yes' or 'no' questions:

- Is it time to focus on your ideas?

- Is it time to rise to the challenge of being authentically you?

- Are you ready to invest in yourself?

If you answered 'yes; to any of those questions, you are ready, let us continue >

If you answered 'no', take more time for yourself but do not wait too long.

77

If you could wave a magic wand and make it happen, describe what you would choose for your life right now.

What are your most important priorities at this time?

Describe how you will manage your priorities in order to begin fulfilling your own dreams.

Where would you like to be and what would you like to be doing with your life and career five years from now?

YOUR ENERGETIC SIGNATURE

When you exit a room, especially a room full of strangers, what atmosphere do you leave behind?

Did your presence contribute to making the room a better environment? Or did it diminish the joy?

You may be able to show your best self to strangers but what about your family?

If your family are important to you, how do you relate to them?

You carry an energetic signature that can be seen in your demeanor and felt by your presence. Are you aware of it and the legacy it leaves behind?

If you are ready to elevate your life, be aware of your interactions and the choices you make every day.

The words that you speak, and the influence of your mind has an effect on your wellbeing, and that of the people around you.

If you are shy and quiet, this is not asking you to be extrovert and outgoing. The quietest person in the room might carry the most beautiful energy that creates a calming environment.

Be childlike, not childish.

Have you ever held a sleeping baby on your chest? What did you experience? What about watching toddlers laugh and having fun? Did those experiences inspire you with more joy?

Children are splendid examples of how we can affect a room. How does it feel when the charming little baby you held in your arms becomes the unruly child throwing a tantrum?

With awareness you can consciously influence your environment, and the feel that remains in a room as you leave. Naturally not everyone will be receptive to you, but those that are, will appreciate the gift of your presence.

Just because someone has an opinion of you does not necessarily make it true but do be honest with yourself and ask if there is any truth in what they say. Sometimes the offence is in how it is said, rather than what is said.

We live in a material world. So money, real estate, and personal possessions matter. The reason they matter is because they can change the circumstances of someone's life.

The most significant legacy you can leave behind is your influence in bringing joy, and in uplifting a person's heart and mind.

Your words and creative work, whether that be in the moment or after your death, mark your success.

The biggest achievement of a lifetime is in how you changed, the ways in which you showed up, the person you become, and in how you inspire the ongoing creation of your life.

Describe what you believe your energy says about you?

Describe what other people say about you?

What, if anything, in your character would you like to change?

In what ways do you bring your larger Being, and the true essence of you into your work?

Describe the reach of your influence and the role you play, for example at church, family, school, or work.

What would you need to do to attain a broader audience for your work?

INTERESTING POINT OF VIEW

Are you open to new ways of thinking, questions, and possibilities?

An open and enquiring mind is vital to creating a joyful life that supports your dreams.

Your mind is a supercomputer, processing information that comes to you from your environment and from the declarations and statements you present to it.

What you say and think can create your life or sabotage it.

Raising children can be demanding. Growing up and navigating the pitfalls of life, the doubts and uncertainties, and the responsibility of life is challenging.

As a parent or teacher your stress, hurt, inadequacy, or fear can easily be communicated to a child and internalized as something wrong with them because babies and children learn by taking in everything around them, what they see, hear, and experience.

What you say matters. What you tell yourself matters. The declarations and statements that you make do matter.

.When overcome with stress, if you speak harshly to your child, remember to right the wrong. Apologize, let them know that you see their beauty and strength, then express your love and appreciation for having them in your life.

Frequent belittling may or may not be actively remembered but the idea remains in the mind. Over time it can undermine their ability to succeed.

Negative judgements can get stuck and operate like a virus below the level of awareness until it seems normal and continues to infiltrate the mind.

If you experience the impact of negative self-talk, learn to become aware of it the moment it surfaces. Adopt the attitude of 'interesting point of view'. Replace negative self-talk with strengthening affirmations.

When you notice negative self-talk ask the following questions conceived by Gary Douglass and Dain Heer of Access Consciousness, 'who does this idea belong to?' followed by "Interesting point of View I have this point of view", followed by "return to sender with consciousness attached". Do not go searching in your mind for answers to those questions or for the actual person the idea belonged to as doing so will drag your mind into more limitation. Allow the thoughts to melt away and for new possibilities to find you.

Access Consciousness provides a clearing statement much like a mantra that can be used to help clear energy that you may not be aware of yet keeps you stuck. A link to the clearing statement can be found on the Success website, see page 312.

By opening your mind to the concept of Interesting Point of View, you open a portal to freedom of thought, freedom to be who you truly be and freedom to live a life mostly designed by you. Mostly because our lives can be affected by the weather, by politics, and by the actions of other people.

We are bombarded with other peoples' opinions. Are you willing to recognize that the thoughts and ideas you cling to about yourself, and about other people are just another interesting point of view?

What are your beliefs about your ability to achieve your dreams?

What statements do you maintain
about your ability to generate money?

QUESTIONS ARE POWERFUL ALLIES

Fixed points of view are a 'dead-end' for ideas, however, the right question opens doorways to new and creative possibilities.

Statements finalize an idea, questions on the other hand invite conversation. A question is a *'what if'* that allows for your awareness to expand to encompass possibilities that previously, you may never have considered.

Questions open up possibilities.
Conclusions and points of view shut
possibilities down.

Do the statements you make to yourself inspire your thinking and create an invitation to other possibilities?

Or does your self-talk shut you down?

Test the idea for yourself...

The invitation to more awareness begins with a question. It empowers you to add your voice to conversation.

There is nothing wrong with statements in the right context but if you want to create greater possibilities, ask a question. For a deeper exploration of your ideas, ask questions. To maintain curiosity about the world, ask questions.

Questions can be uncomfortable because they are normally used to summon a response. Do not be afraid to ask the right question at the right time and do not feel that you have to respond to every probing demand.

According to Gary Douglass of access Consciousness, a fixed idea with a question mark attached, is not a real question, for example "*why am I so useless at* _____*?"*. This is not a real question. It is a limiting point of view.

Try this instead, "*what would it take for me to be exceptional at* _____*?"*

Here are a few questions to assist you:-

- When life is going well ask - *'How does it get any better than this?'*

- When life is not going well ask - *'How does it get any better than this?*

- When you are in the middle of a stressful situation ask - *What else is possible?*

So now, what else is possible?

Make a note below of existing
possibilities that you would like to explore.

STRONG INTENTION & BOLD ACTION

Strong intention with bold action brings ideas to life. Do you have a plan of action for bringing your ideas to life?

If not, get one now!

If yes, are you implementing it?

Are you reviewing and assessing your goals on a regular basis to ensure they align with your long-term vision?

Are your dreams big enough to carry your life forward to higher levels of personal fulfillment?

Focus your thoughts on your first step, then take the next step and the step after that, which of course, is also a first step. It is the first time you have taken that breath and the first time you have been alive living that moment.

Think about the first time you were successful at anything, a competition, a race, or even a quiz or game. What set the scene for that success?

It was your intention to do the best you could and take whatever steps were needed to reach your goal. You no doubt enjoyed yourself and the idea of failure did not cross your mind. Your desire to win took precedence over fear and anxiety.

Do the following:-

- Prepare your mind by making quiet time for reflection
- Set dates in your diary to mark a commitment to follow through
- Affirm your intentions by taking action
- Take note of the signposts that appear along the way

If you remain focused, committed to your goal, and give your best, the outcome happens on its own.

The magic is in the journey.

Life will always present things that are outside of your control. It will continue to teach you if you are willing to learn.

Life as we say happens. It gives you material to inspire your creativity. It is up to you to imaginatively shape what you have and manifest something, out of nothing.

Stand up for and stand behind your ideas

We all have moments when we would prefer to run away and hide rather than face a challenge but how does that affect your life?

Decide ahead of time that you will stay and fight for your dream. Take your first stride, all other steps will follow.

Do your goals align with your values?

If you accept the challenges that your life presents, if you work consistently and with true diligence, if you turn up every day despite your fears, you increase the potential for your dreams to manifest into reality.

Grab a pen, state your intentions on the following pages, then allow innovative ideas, new insights, and new habits to form.

What do you intend to create this year?

What new philosophies or ideas do you choose to embrace?

What contribution will you make to your family and friends,

What contribution will you make to your local community

What contribution will you make to the world at large

STATEMENT OF INTENT

Today's Date_____

   I, _____ **commit**
this year to exploring my creativity.

   I will be watchful and monitor my thoughts so that I recognize the negative self-talk that puts me down and stops me from moving forward. I will use daily affirmations and other tools to improve my thoughts. I will train my mind and my body for success.

   During the next 12 months I intend to carry out the actions described on the subsequent pages:-

   I will not waver, and I will not fail. I will bring my best to ensure success.

Signed _____ **Dated** _____

What do you intend to initiate over the next 6 months?

Month	Single goal / action
January	
February	
March	
April	
May	
June	

State a simple goal or action for each of the following months.

Month	Single goal / action
July	
August	
September	
October	
November	
December	

THE WISDOM IN FAILURE

Award winning artists, designers, inventors, entrepreneurs, athletes, scientists, and people from all levels of society and professions failed multiple times before success.

There is much to be learned from failure

Many of the technologies and innovations that you use in your home and at work started out as failures but were redesigned to become essential products, one example of this is sticky notepads. The glue was too weak for its initial purpose but added to small pieces of paper it continues to sell by the billions each year.

Your project or task may have failed but you are not a failure. You may have made the decision yourself to stop, or you may have been forced to discontinue your efforts by circumstances beyond your control. That does NOT make YOU a failure. The situation changed, a choice was made, a decision taken.

If the project failed because you miscalculated, then gather your information, reflect on the cause but do not destroy your worth because of the outcome. Who knows, depending on your reasons for quitting, you might decide to pick up and continue at a later date.

Failure is a great teacher if you are a willing student and choose to learn

If your project failed, embrace the idea that it was one step on the way to success and expertise. Nobody seeks to fail but failure provides valuable knowledge that you will not get from a straight success.

If you decide to resume your project, you might course-correct and find a solution.

Procrastination though is different because delay can cause a project to fail before it has even started.

Do you find multiple reasons to not get started, to not do the thing?

Are you the type of person that talks yourself out of something before trying it?

Do you tend to hold pessimistic points of view?

Do you often put yourself down and doubt your ability?

Remember that Skill development and proficiency do not happen overnight, but as a result of sustained practice.

Think of failure as a test of your idea and an education in how to do it better the next try around.

RISK MITIGATION

Do not give energy to pondering whether or not you will succeed, maintain an expectation that you will flourish and do a risk assessment.

If you know your risks, rather than abandoning an idea, you can mitigate against them or choose to go in a different direction.

It is ok to change your mind but own it. Do it with awareness. Do not' blame somebody else for your choice. Release the energy bound up in blame, into focusing on what you are aiming to achieve.

Use the questions on the following pages to assist you in assessing the risks to your project then complete the risk assessment form on page 116

Make a list of reasons why you cannot start your new endeavor and why your plans could go wrong.

Make a list of things you could do to reduce the impact of what could potentially go wrong...

On the next page copy your list and against each item note what is needed to take care of the issue so that it becomes non-existent, or the risk minimized.

Risk Mitigation Form

	Risk	Corrective action
1.		
2.		
3.		
4.		
5.		
6.		
7.		

The activity you just completed is a simple risk assessment. It can help you decide your next step.

SELF REFLECTION

What new skills do you now have and
what new awareness have you
received?

To have an extraordinary
life, step outside your
comfort zone

Section Four

YOU ARE MORE THAN ENOUGH

Intelligence is not just intellectual. There are many types of intelligence, and intelligence to life itself. A universal organizing force that enables the seasons to change, the planets to revolve and all of life, as we know it, to function smoothly.

This Intelligence exists within your DNA. It creates the ability for a tiny cell, invisible to the naked eye, to develop and grow into human form. This innate intelligence gives you the ability to breathe without conscious effort.

Try holding your breath for a brief period of time, You cannot use willpower to hold your breath until all life is gone because your lifeforce will reassert control.

If intelligence is embedded in every cell of your body, then no matter your intellectual ability, how can you not be capable and worthy of achieving remarkable things.

This section is about generating confidence in your abilities and your worth. It is about you becoming more confident to show up in the world on purpose.

Your body has intelligence that you did not have to study for. Your body is a living genius and with a bit of effort, everyone can acquire a skill or talent that can be shared in unique ways

You have the capacity for greatness and a talent to offer that can be expressed in ways unique to YOU!

No matter how you were conceived, no matter how you came into this world or how you now live in this world, you are not a mistake. Remember that intelligence is embedded into your DNA. Your job is to step forward and bring your talents.

What causes you to be afraid of sharing your talents with other people?

Describe the skill or talent you would most like to share that you have been too afraid to present?

If you chose to present your work to an audience, describe what it would be and to whom you would show it.

NO LONGER A SLAVE TO THE MIND

Have you witnessed the power and grace of a top athlete?

Have you observed the focus that allows them to be fully present in the moment? If so, you have seen how the mind can assist the body.

Your mind is a tool of infinite potential that can be used to create greater possibilities.

Athletes learn to give complete attention to the task at hand. They train the body and still the mind of its negative chatter in order for the body to take control and complete the task for which it has been drilled.

Your brain is a supercomputer, a processor of information whose job it is to help you make sense of your physical world and respond to stimuli. Studies show that the more athletes think about what they must do, the less likely they are to succeed.

If your mind is the queen of your world, she will lead you astray.

You may not want to become a professional athlete, but the same principle of training your mind and body to obey your command can help you to become mistress, rather than slave to your thoughts. See the following pages for ideas on training the mind.

Mindfulness training

- Set clear goals
- Create routines and habits that help you to focus your time and keep you on track
- Review your progress against your measure of success by keeping a journal
- Monitor your self-talk.
- Spend time Imagining yourself in the position, place, business, job, or dream life.
- Visualize and imagine yourself reaching your goal
- Go through the motions of reaching your goal
- Celebrate ahead of time
- Speak positive affirmations of your ability to succeed at it, whatever it is

- Practice deep breathing exercises to oxygenate the body and clear the mind
- Meditate
- Flex, stretch and tone your body
- Flex, stretch and tone your mind
- Dress to improve your confidence

How might applying the practice and discipline used by top athletes help you overcome your fear of showing up in the world larger than you are now?

WHAT AWARENESS IS LIFE OFFERING

The great scientist, Albert Einstein said that you cannot solve a problem from the same viewpoint as the problem itself, or words to that effect.

If the only thing you see in your life are problems, you will not notice the solution right in front of you.

'Bad' things can happen to anyone, including good people, but you do not have to be a victim of circumstances all of your life.

If you make excuses, how will you be able to receive assistance from others?

If you are in denial, how will you recognize what needs to change?

As Wayne Dyer stated, there is a spiritual solution to every problem. There is more to your life and the circumstances that have brought you thus far, than you currently comprehend.

Do not make excuses.
Take action and make preparations
for the future you are working
towards

Often the solution to a problem can be found in the problem itself.

The discomfort you feel is a call to a greater life. It is YOU pushing you to take action.

Will you choose now to fully embrace the possibilities that life offers? What does that mean? It means no longer seeing yourself as a victim. It means venturing out to places that you have never been to before, meeting people that you have never met before, saying yes to possibilities, accepting responsibility for your life and taking action. Doing this enables you each day to become a greater version of yourself than you were the day before.

Make a note of where you have been procrastinating?

Describe how implementing the
ideas you find here might change your life?

What have you been unwilling to acknowledge up until now?

EMBRACE THE STRUGGLE

Human beings are lazy.... We want comfort and ease. Unless inspired and with strong motivation, most people will not move beyond comfort, they lack the discipline to carry ideas to fruition.

If you did not experience the heaviness or struggle you may be going through right now, would you really do anything to change your life?

Your struggles are a message from Big You to little you

The unease and longing for something more is a wakeup call to an adventure. Emotional distress, physical pain, boredom, or grumbling is a small voice calling you out, then SHOUTING at you... TIME TO WAKE UP!

The more you rationalize your unease, it will periodically surface until you do something about it.

You might try to distract yourself with work, games, social media, or television. You might try to alleviate emotional distress with drugs, sex, food, or addictive behaviors, but you cannot hide from yourself.

Discomfort, whether physical or emotional, is a way of waking you up and letting you know that it is time to take action.

Life will continue to draw your attention to the fact that it is time for you to make a change. It calls for meaningful reflection. It demands that you engage in a greater exploration of your health, who you truly be and what contribution you

could make to a wider audience than just
to the person in the mirror. To an audience
bigger than one person.

If you are meddling in someone
else's life, you are not fully present for your
own.

Where are you not fully present in
your life?

Is it time now for you to

become a creator rather

than just a consumer?

CONSUMER VS CREATOR

Are you more aware and more creative than your family and friends?

Does your sensitivity make you self-absorbed and self-centered or do you use that ability to contribute to others?

Where could you be of service to others but are not showing up to fulfil the promise of you?

Your setbacks and disappointments are opportunities to break through the fairytales and illusions that keep you doing things in the exact same way that you have always done.

Are you following a path set by someone else just because you are afraid to disappoint?

Authenticity is beautiful. What is real and genuine cannot be hidden. The things about you that are different to everyone else are what makes you unique. Are you willing to be different?

Are you ready to find you?

Are you ready to be a transformation agent?

If so, time to step up.

You can buy all kinds of things online, but you cannot order a new body or a new life, You must bring into existence what you desire and do it for yourself.

You can continue to just consume what other people produce, or you can become a creator yourself, conveying ideas and influence. What will you choose?

What are you good at making?

What topics are you passionate about?

What skills or innate talent could you turn into a product that someone else might want?

SHOW UP ON PURPOSE

Everything you see around you, including you, was once just an idea.

As a child, were you told to stop daydreaming?

The most inventive minds daydream, reflect and contemplate. Your reveries and desires form the seeds of future creations.

Your beliefs and ideas create reality

Are you looking for a career change? Do you have a new product idea?

If you are working to improve your relationships or your health, if there is a song inside you waiting to be written, if you are waiting to finish your education, whatever you can create, begins with a dream, a vision or simple idea.

Do the people around you appear indifferent in the face of your enthusiasm?

Do they display a lack of faith in you or your ideas? How about this idea, do not listen to them.

This does not mean shutting out constructive feedback but refuse to entertain negative beliefs that would have you think you are of no worth. Challenge every thought that would put you down. Actively make time for positive contemplation.

Spend some time every day in contemplation. Do it to embed new thoughts and ideas into your life. Do it every day and let it carry you one step closer every day to your goal.

Do not allow your brilliant idea to become another uncompleted task that creates anxiety, leads to disappointment, and adds to your to-do list.

The more time you commit to taking action, the more eager you will be to keep the energy moving and look forward to getting back to a project that has potential to transform your life.

Start by committing at least 15 minutes every day to journaling your thoughts. Show up consistently and eventually it will feel like second nature. See page 311 for other journals in this series.

Open up to your new practice. Allow yourself to be inspired, even dazzled by your brilliance and the extent of your creative thought.

A few Ideas on taking action

- Actively seek out people, communities or groups that inspire you

- Find practices that help you manage your emotions and how you feel about them

- Engage in creative pursuits

  Where are you holding back from being the contribution you could truly be?

  Describe the commitment you will make today to create a practice of Taking Action?

No matter what age you are right now, you have the rest of your life in front of you... so go ahead... Live your best life, despite your limitations

VIVACIOUS AGEING. MAKE IT FUN!

From birth to death the physical body is in an ongoing process of transformation. Billions of cells die and are replaced every day. Each part of your body has its own lifecycle. Some cells are replaced every few weeks, other cells take years

Everybody ages and youthful years speed past quicker than expected, but life and living are not just for the young. No matter what age you are right now, you still have the rest of your life ahead of you.

The following pages are for women of every age. It is for women entering middle and senior years also for the younger woman, because the young, do not stay young forever.

Mature women possess a resilience that comes from having lived through the storms of life, having loved, and lost, faced financial difficulties, sleepless nights, raised children, and be alive to tell their stories.

Despite the pervasive Hollywood ideal of slim, youthful bodies, the mature female body exhibits a sensual, authentic self-assurance.

Remember that true wisdom is a valuable asset

If emotionally mature, senior women long ago transitioned beyond teenage self-consciousness, she overcame the need to conform, and is much more aware about who she is, and what she wants.

Sexual capacity and sexual desire may change but much to the surprise of younger people, the desire for sexual pleasure is not over. Despite slow down or chronic health issues, mature women can still have fun with her remaining years. She might even be surprised at the appeal she presents to younger men.

To age with grace and vigor be open to living as fully as you are able

Active seniors in the ninth and tenth decade of life continue to have aspirations for themselves, their children, and dream projects awaiting completion.

As you age, your body will change in unexpected ways. It will take more effort to maintain your health, strength, and appearance, and it may take more focus to complete tasks, but life still has the potential to surprise. You can either let life just happen to you or give it space to happen for you. You have to give yourself a reason to keep living.

Make a commitment to maintain your strength and suppleness so that you can live a full and productive life. Here are some ideas for aging vivaciously:-

- Look at life through the eyes of a grandchild to help you appreciate its wonders,

- Pay attention to the foods you eat as quality nutrition is one of the cornerstones of good health.

- Foster social contacts that support you through challenging times.

- Despite new constraints, think about how to travel comfortably.

- Join groups and find new activities

- Be inventive

- Ensure that you move your body on a regular basis, to maintain flexibility of mind as well as body.

- As a positive contribution to the people around you look for ways each day to express gratitude,

- Focus on what works well for you,

- Listen to stories of seniors who defy the odds by achieving significant goals in senior years (see footnote [2])

---

[2] **Focus on vivacious ageing:** The '*Growing Bolder*' podcast focuses on the achievements of people during senior years. See growingbolder.com

The Senior Games Association promotes the benefits of competitive sports, physical fitness & active aging to adults age 50+ yrs. See nsga.com

What would you do and have at this stage in your life?

What can you incorporate into your daily life in order to experience life at its fullest.

SELF REFLECTION

What new skills do you now have and what new awareness have you received?

No matter what happens,
you are not a failure.

If you get up and keep
going, failure becomes the
test run for better

Section Five

YOU BECOME YOUR BELIEFS

This section will assist you to examine the unconscious thoughts that pervade your day and sabotage your success.

Beliefs are the collective thoughts, attitudes, customs, and ideas ingrained in you by your society and the influence of the people around you during your formative years.

Those beliefs become deeply embedded and reinforced. They shape your thoughts and beliefs, and whether you are fully aware of them or not, they shape your life.

Each time you validate a belief, whether positive or negative, you reinforce it. Eventually it becomes part of your habitual thinking and informs your perception of life and other people.

Your beliefs offer a sense of identity, and you can find shelter in belonging to a community but to craft your success, you have to let go of beliefs that do not support it.

In order to release undermining beliefs, you first have to know the harmful thoughts that exist inside you. This can be uncomfortable.

To put this into context, Are you blessed to live in a country where your freedom of expression is protected? If yes, why remain imprisoned by your mind?

Are you in control of your mind and emotions or are they in control of you?

A woman with courage whose freedom is restricted by her government, can live a powerful, and impassioned life if she has purpose.

Time, energy, and life do not stand still. They flow. Life is fluid. There was a time in human history when the earth was believed to be flat. Now we know otherwise. Nothing in nature is solidly fixed. You are part of the natural world, Work on letting go of thoughts and ideas that do not allow your life to encompass your joyful expression of life.

What thoughts do you maintain about your ability to succeed?

Using your notes from the previous page turn the ideas about your ability to succeed into positive affirmations that support success. Use the space below to work it out and note them down.

PERCEPTION, REALITY & TRUTH

Universal truths maintain the natural environment but the material, transactional world that we occupy operates on perception.

Since everyone's perceptions differ in one way or another, it could be said that reality is the illusion we create with other people, about life.

Your perception, thoughts, actions, and reactions are products of your beliefs but your way of seeing or the way you were taught to interpret the world, is only one view of the world. Other people are equally convinced of their opinions and beliefs.

When the life you are living runs counter to the life you want or counter to your embedded beliefs, the result is inner conflict.

Neal Donald Walsh in his book
"*When Everything Changes, Change*
Everything", describes 3 levels of reality

- Ultimate Reality

- Observed Reality

- Distorted Reality

    Leading to:

- Actual Truth

- Apparent Truth

- Imagined Truth

    All thoughts, good' and 'bad' are
projections that can either hold you in
fear of the future or release you to greater
possibilities. To the windsurfer, a blustery
day seems glorious; to the picnicker it may
not. To a sun lover, tropical heat is
magnificent, to those preferring a
temperate climate, it is not.

Do you cling to your point of view, whether it is right or wrong, just because it is yours?

Are you judge, jury, and executioner?

Your thoughts about someone make it true for you but does not necessarily mean it is the truth. You see what you want to believe, hence your perception of reality may be quite different to the actual truth.

How often do you project your past onto your current life and use it to invalidate your present experiences?

How often do you point a finger rather than look in the mirror? If you spend time scrutinizing other peoples' behavior, then you are not spending enough time reflecting on your own.

The more judgments you hold, the more blind you are to your own conduct.

Indian religions highlight the idea of cause and effect. Everything you do has a ripple effect that eventually finds its way back to you. If you do good, you will be rewarded with good; if you do terrible things to other people then the bad will equally find its way back to you. They call this karma.

Every judgement bears a consequence, every action a karmic seed. What seeds are you sowing?

In the West we say, 'what goes around comes back around'. You are a work in progress as is everyone else. Examine your thoughts and motivations but do not negate yourself for having them. Stand up for yourself, look for solutions, and address the behavior. Do not attempt to destroy the person in order to make yourself feel better, and that includes yourself.

How do you feel about people who hold ideas that are different to yours?

In a world that has become more diverse, who are the people that you want your work to speak to?

CATCH YOUR THOUGHTS

We use only ten percent of the brain's capacity but mostly clutter it with pettiness, judgements against the world, and inconsequential ideas. In fact, most thought focuses on bygone hurts, and past failures. Most thoughts are a waste of the powerful energy the brain possesses.

Modern life requires less use of our survival mechanisms and more use of intellectual aptitude and ability to think clearly.

Constantly focusing on what is not working puts the body under stress and primes the body's survival instincts. It begins by shutting down non-essential activities in order to conserve energy for fight or flight. It diverts energy towards the muscles in your torso, arms and legs readying you for action, and diverts energy away from the higher faculties in the brain needed for critical thinking. Living with constant stress affects your ability to make good decisions.

It is important that you pay attention to how your mind operates because success is fueled by a disciplined mind.

Your mind needs guidance, inspiration and to be presented with fresh, insightful information. You cannot afford an undisciplined mind.

Thoughts hold power over your life. They affect your actions, reactions, and outcomes. Refuse to entertain negative beliefs that would have you think that you are of no worth.

Becoming aware of your thoughts and Interrupting patterns of thinking that serves no real purpose other than to make you feel bad begins to powerfully transform your life.

Your body does not function well for prolonged periods of time on poor food and little sleep. Your mind also needs to be nourished and nurtured in order to play a positive role in creating the life you would choose to live.

Are you aware of the conversations that take place in your mind when you are not actively thinking about a particular topic?

Take a moment to catch just one of your repetitive thoughts. What did you find? Was it uplifting, peaceful and contented? Was it judgmental, self-loathing, or full of recrimination and gossip?

Do you allow your thoughts to trick you into believing that you are unworthy, and need be in fear of stepping out of your comfort zone and trying something new?

The next time you are alone, catch one of your thoughts. Put the thought into words and describe it on the following pages. If it generates a feeling, describe the feeling.

What do you think about the most?

What beliefs do you hold that limit your ability to positively carry your life forward?

CHANGE YOUR THOUGHTS

Thoughts and ideas shape the reality you perceive. They assert an influence on your health, your demeanor, and the successful outcome of your goals. Thoughts that dominate your mind shape your world.

Consider how you feel when depressed and how difficult it is to pull yourself out of feelings of hopelessness and judgment.

Your brain is extraordinary, As you think, connections are created via neural pathways that channel information.

Like the rest of the body, the brain is naturally programmed to use the most efficient, resourceful, and effective means to carry out its functions and maintain your mental capacity. Once it establishes a pathway, it uses the same route again when presented with similar information. Thoughts of a similar kind cause an idea to become ingrained into a firm belief about yourself and the world around you.

Thoughts magnetize other thoughts

When depressed, you are likely to feel more depressed, when angry you form more angry thoughts until something breaks the pattern. Your perceptions are also affected by your internal state, how you feel on any given day.

Your depressed moods are a mix of chemicals in the brain, which can be altered by natural or pharmaceutical methods.

The following page presents some non-medical approaches that may help to make a change in how you feel Remember that if you have psychiatric concerns or cannot cope effectively with everyday life, please consult a medical professional.

Simple stress-reduction tools

- Exercise

- Yoga

- Breathwork

- Herbs and plants such as: Ashwagandha, lavender, chamomile, kava kava, valerian, St John's Wort (discuss potential contraindications with your doctor before use)

- Wholesome food

- Counselling and psychotherapy

Become attentive to your emotions, notice your breathing, monitor your thought process, and actively break the judgements you have about yourself.

Bruce Lipton in his book "*Biology of Belief*" asserts that your thoughts can affect the microscopic building blocks of the human genes.

The author and metaphysis, Richard Rudd discusses what he calls *Gene Keys*, an inner language designed to communicate directly with your DNA.

He believes that every human being is born with the potential for brilliance with the code for genius imprinted within the DNA of every cell at conception.

Rudd states that DNA is highly sensitive to electromagnetic fields, and that every thought, feeling, and activity instantly generates a magnetic imprint that gets communicated to all other cells in the body. He asserts that under a microscope, DNA can be seen to contract under low frequencies, and conversely, expand with higher frequencies.

He suggests that low frequency thoughts or negative emotions cause DNA to begin shutting down higher faculties linked to mental processing and that words and thoughts can change those frequencies. If this is true then thoughts and affirmations holding the energy of expansion and joy can change your life for the better,

Change your thoughts, change your DNA, change your life

The more you practice gratitude, recalling joyful memories, and finding appreciation for what you have rather than bemoaning what you do not have, the better you will feel about yourself and enjoy even more positive experiences.

We are creatures of habit. It takes at least a month, approximately 30 days of committed, consistent, daily practice to begin changing habitual patterns of thinking. Use the following ideas to get you started:-

Self-awareness practices

- Become aware of your thoughts and interrupt negative patter by turning it around to look for the opposite

- Reflect on memories that uplift you.

- Start a practice of daily meditation and reflection

- Learn energy cultivation practices such as chi gong and tai chi

- Celebrate your wins with rewards

- Get a mentor

- Book an Access Bars session visit www.createayearofsuccess.com for more information

Question the ideas you hold. about
yourself. Do they give rise to thoughts that
affirm, nurture, support, and allow you to
grow, and manifest in a positive way? Or do
they add to your burdens, bringing doubt,
insecurity and undermine your success?

Challenge every thought that would
put you down.

Intellect and thought help us carry
tasks through to completion but the
greatest inventions, the most beautiful
creations and momentous events that
changed the world, were fueled by
imagination.

A few ideas to nurture your mind

- Eat clean, chemical free food

- Drink clean water

- Active daily movement for both mind & body

- Watch, read and listen to Inspirational books, movies & audio

- Stretch your body and your mind

- Dream beyond current reality

- Get inquisitive to continue learning

- Switch off the television

- Do puzzles, crosswords, and games

- Get a good night's sleep every night

What other ideas do you have for changing the pattern of your thoughts and nurturing your mind?

YOUR PAST VS YOUR FUTURE

We live, breathe, eat, sleep, walk, and talk about our personal histories. Our stories offer meaning when life feels empty and bring comfort when emotionally bereft.

In our stories we reveal our joys, but more often our frustrations, woes, and suffering. We invest time, effort, and energy in their telling and re-telling.

You may not forget hurtful past experiences, but your past need not be your future.

YOUR memory is but ONE perception of the past.

Are you continuing to learn, adapt, and grow or are you just repeating history?

Rather than be driven by old stories that would have you thinking less of yourself, outpace them. Release what has gone and cannot be undone, let go of what does not work, think instead about making your life authentically yours.

Are you evolving or are you just repeating history?

How often do you grumble? How many times per day do you complain about your life? How regularly do you express gratitude?

Stories freeze time. Constant complaining hinders the freedom and joyful expression of life. Endless recounting of painful memories binds you to the past.

Revisiting thoughts that hurt you will never fix the hurt or change your analysis of them.

Your personal narrative may seem to provide satisfaction and validation of your hurt feelings, but it becomes a mantra that fosters negative thoughts, feeds fear and leads to more resentment.

The controlling character of human beings, often referred to as the ego, is the conscious, decision-making part of the mind. It tries to protect you but can frustrate your efforts to reach the fullest version of what you could achieve.

There is a time to speak and a time to listen and be silently consoled

An unhealthy ego uses your stories to justify anger. It convinces you that your perception of a hurtful situation, although it may do little to alleviate your problems, is evidence enough to sustain your devotion to the hurt.

Consistent complaining month shadowing month, year after year, disempowers you, and fatigues those who listen.

This is not to say that you should not speak about your troubles. Voicing your concerns can lead to solutions, it can help bring calm to a fraught situation. In confessing your regrets there is potential for rectifying a hurt and for reconciliation and healing to begin.

When you are truly heard you feel empowered, but by losing track of the story, you miss how quickly time passes.

The past does not have the power to change your future.

Time does not stand still. The years slip away. Your judgmental mind will not resolve past regrets, merely ensures your pain does not leave.

Emotional pain is rooted to a memory anchored in past experiences yet has the ability to trigger pain in the present. Painful memories stored in your body can lead to stress and ill health.

If you have grown and matured, you are no longer the person you were back in that initial moment of hurt. The characters in your story may have changed or moved away, but your constant scrutiny keeps them alive, present in your life.

Old stories keep you tenured to a memory you might rather forget.

Only by letting go of the past do you become the person you might wish to be, the person you have not yet met.

When you release the toxic effects of hurt, you may remember the story, but it becomes a recounting of what influenced your transformation rather than an emotional trigger that causes more pain.

What personal stories do you focus on with great regularity?

What can you do to shift your focus from the past to the present?

YOU ARE AMAZING

You do not have to tell every cell in your body what to do, so how do you manage to get through the day intact?

Because you are amazing!

If you have difficulty believing this, just consider how efficiently you manage to keep breathing, to move your limbs, or to perform any of the tasks you ask your body to undertake. How do you do it?

Do your ideas about you match who you truly be?

How do you manage to keep pumping blood through your heart or oxygen into your lungs?

How do you manage to effortlessly co-ordinate the billions of neurons that engage to lift a pen, light a fire, chop food without chopping off a finger? How do you manage to get the cup to your lips correctly with the right time, speed, and dexterity to drink a hot beverage?

Your body knows what to do. Once you have gained dexterity you do not have to think about the action. When you have an idea, in an instant you can carry out an action to achieve what you had in mind. Your thought to open a door causes an automatic response in the body. Somehow your brain converts thought into action, an idea into something real with measurable effects. Your mind readily produces what you think about.

Your mind, body, and spirit work together to sustain life.

Which part of the mind would you say has the most influence, the conscious or the unconscious mind?

The conscious mind makes a statement, and the unconscious mind fulfils it as a request. The conscious mind makes judgements, the unconscious mind accepts them as true. The unconscious mind serves the requests of the conscious mind. The conscious mind asks the questions, the unconscious mind carries out the request.

Your mind is lush and abundant in its potential to generate amazing and ingenious creations.

Your conscious mind must lead the way to cultivating and maintaining a happier state of mind. In other words, the answers to your problems are not outside of your control.

Describe some amazing facts about yourself. Start by enthusiastically describing the features of your face. If you find that difficult imagine that you are describing a friend.

CREATE YOUR REALITY

The sun, the wind and the rain do what they do. A beautiful day for one person is misery for the other. Whose reality is true?

Which version of the day is the distortion, and which is the real thing?

Reality is subjective and your mental processing is what makes something real to you.

For good or bad the standards, attitudes and ideas learned in early life become part of your value system and can control your behavior decades later.

Your beliefs and values assert a strong influence on your interaction with other people, especially your intimate relationships and work colleagues.

Judgmental attitudes undermine relationships.

There are many versions of reality and other people may not accept your 'truth' as right for them. It may not fit their version of the world.

Why does this matter? Because success is built on relationships and the impact you have on other people.

In building relationships remember that it is easier to influence others when you respect their right to their own opinion, even if it is different to yours, than by using the force of your character to coerce them into accepting your point of view.

Intimidation grants only short-term results yet has long-term implications for relationships.

What would you ask of life right now, at this time in your life?

In what ways would you like your reality to change?

What is the most important thing you would like to manifest within the next year?

What can you do to make that happen?

What beliefs do you hold that do not positively carry your life forward?

Turn those ideas into a positive active statement

SELF REFLECTION

What new skills do you now have and what new awareness have you received?

Your favorite distractions,
whether demands from other
people or social media,
consume your time and take
you away from your decision
to grow beyond your current
reality.

Protect your time!

Section Six

DITCH THE DRAMA

Humans love drama. People love people watching, and the crazier it gets, the more people watch. We watch it on television, we see it in movies, we get engrossed in it on the daily news, we even create it in our lives.

Become aware of the drama that runs your life. Knowing this will give you greater strength to choose what is right for you.

This section will look at

- Your feelings and emotions
- Your emotional triggers.
- Your fears and how to grow beyond them

Are you ready to ditch the drama? >

EMOTIONAL TRIGGERS

Are you aware of your emotional triggers?

This is when a current disagreement causes an emotional outburst that may not have originated with the person with whom you disagree, but a result of other events in the past that you have projected onto this person

Did a recent incident trigger the memory of a past hurt?

Deep inside you sense what a good relationship is, and you know whether or not this is one of them.

Do not tolerate abuse. Do not make excuses for ill treatment. Walk away, in fact, run for your life. Learn from your experience.

If an abusive relationship left you feeling inconsequential, if you experienced invalidation by a narcissistic parent and were not given the freedom or opportunity to express your own emotions, ask yourself, are the emotions associated with those early events now playing themselves out with new characters?

Use the following questions as prompts to reflect on your relationship.

- Is this a temporary hitch in the relationship?
- What positive influences does this relationship offer you ?
- Is it time to walk away?
- Do you have the strength to walk away?
- If not, can you set a time limit to learn new skills and gather the strength to create a better life?

- When you fall into moments of self-invalidation, do not beat yourself up, instead ask the following questions:

- Who or what does this belong to?

- What can I do about this?

- What is the real trigger for these emotions?

- Am I facing my issues or projecting onto someone else?

- What am I ignoring?

- What have I been unwilling to acknowledge?

- How can I use this to improve my life?

- How much allowance can I have for myself

- In recognizing that we are all different, how much allowance can I find inside me for this person and this moment?

Knowing your triggers does not mean that you should accept unkind or unjust behavior. You have the right to say what works for you. Speak and allow your voice to be heard. If you cannot communicate with this person, then perhaps it is time to reconsider how much of your time you give to this relationship.

Sometimes, your closest people may not understand or agree with your choices, they may not support you or 'stand in your corner'. Remember, other people's ideas about you are just an interesting point of view and they have their own issues.

Do not align and identify with belittling ideas, Do not adopt them as your own. You do not have to respond, react, or be pulled further into drama. Find compassion for the little girl inside of you who really desires to be hugged.

Recognition of your emotional triggers will give you greater freedom in choosing what is right for you. This moment is an opportunity to reclaim yourself.

Describe what you are experiencing right now?

DREAM KILLERS

Be aware of the blessing and curse of those who know you well, or what Julie McNamee in "The Artists Way" describes as Crazy Makers. This applies to individuals, who on the one hand appear to celebrate you. They may open doors, and create opportunities for you, but at the same time take pleasure in being destructive and interrupting your success when you make noteworthy progress.

Crazy makers as described by Julie McNamee are people who find ways to burst your bubble and deter you from moving forward. They do this using many methods, including:

- Emotional blackmail
- Anger
- Resentment
- Drama

- Put downs

Anyone that creates confusion and drama at the point where you have decided to change your life, can be regarded as a Crazy Maker. You might even be your own Crazy Maker.

Recognize that these people test your commitment to growth. They recognize your talent but unfortunately are also aware of your weaknesses. Though they may appear to validate you, they are also amongst the first to put you down and point out your weakness because it makes them feel powerful.

Do not leave part of yourself behind or take any of their invalidation by engaging with their negativity. Stand up for yourself and make a greater commitment to your success. Shift your focus from them into positive action toward your goals.

When Crazy Makers see you are no longer willing to waste your time or energy, they will either leave you alone or take a different attitude.

Your job is to work on your own issues and question your own crazy making behavior.

Time is short

Find your rhythm

Keep choosing

Maintain focus

Do not allow your focus to
shift.

Keep going...!

ACKNOWLEDGE YOUR DISCOMFORT

How often do you wake up feeling lousy, then let it rule your entire day?

Do your feelings tell you who you are?

Feelings are fleeting. When you claim the feelings and emotions as who you are. If you hold onto them for extended periods of time, wrap them into your identity, and do not recognize their transitory nature, they maintain a hold on you.

Feelings act like a barometer. They provide information about the emotional effects of your thinking and an indicator of how you are affected by your environment and the people around you.

The amount of time that negative emotions stay heightened and linger inside

213

you, can undermine not only your health but your ability to realize your dreams.

How long does it take you to recover from upsets?

Your emotions represent the conflict between body and mind, the physical and the spiritual, the seen and unseen. They reveal your perception of reality at a point in time.

Struggle and discomfort are a normal part of human experience.

If you want to be free from the grip of negative emotions, take a bird's eye view. This means stepping back from the moment, let the intensity subside, and dispassionately observe what is taking place.

Think about the following; If you are angry and your assessment of a situation turns out to be incorrect, would it have been worth the upset? Would the action you are about to take be morally or legally defensible?

As discussed in a previous chapter, you may not be upset for the reasons you think at the time. When an unpleasant experience is embedded as part of your emotional identity and self-talk It continues to trigger you.

Can you accept that you will sometimes 'feel bad' and experience moments of discomfort?

In your relationships do you behave in any of the following ways?

- Are you pushing away and rejecting when what you want is to be held?

- Are you the first to attack because you are afraid of being attacked and want to ensure you are on top?
- Are you always ready to argue and fight?
- Are you in the habit of reacting first, thinking later, then not liking the effects?

Emotions are part of being human. You may not like them, but you will continue to face them. You will also cause emotional grief to somebody else either intentionally or unintentionally. Learning to manage uncomfortable emotions will give you stability.

You may not forget a hurt, but you do not have to carry the wound throughout your life. It does not have an automatic right to exist in your present time.

Be present, be proactive, set goals
that will help you reclaim your life.

What is the most frequent emotion you experience on a day-to-day basis at this point in your life?

What are your habitual reactions?

MAKE PEACE WITH THE PAST

If you make a mistake, then make amends, offer solace, an apology, right the wrong in whichever way you can.

Learn from guilt but do not let it waste your life. Where you need to change, allow it to help you do that. Become an inspiration but do not let guilt destroy you.

Make peace with your past. Let go of the idea that it has power over you. Bring your mind into the present and try to live each day, fully in the present.

What have you done in the past that you now regret?

Who did you hurt in the past to whom you owe an apology?

What do you need to do to fully make amends?

What will give you peace of mind?

Let your highest self,
become the mistress of your
mind.

DO NOT GIVE IN TO FEAR

There are real dangers in this world that require us to be alert and aware. Fear is the signal that we should pay attention to our environment as danger may be nearby.

There are women living in regions of conflict and war that live in constant fear of sexual violence, terrified for the safety of their family and for themselves, yet they have no choice but to venture out onto dangerous streets in order to find food.

A recent broadcast about the war in Sudan by the BBC World Service, recounted the story of a mother offering herself to the militia in place of her young daughters. She chose to save her girls from the horror of rape and possibly murder.

Bad people do exist, terrible things do happen, and there is good reason to be alert to danger, but most of us are not exposed to that level of danger and daily trauma.

The reason for drawing attention to that story is to help you put your fears into context. Despite increasing conflict throughout the world, many people live in a bubble of safety and relative privilege, yet the mind can conjure fear where there is no present danger.

The media bombards us with sensational news, negative stories, and strong opinions about other people.

We are disturbed by noise from a variety of sources and electromagnetic devices that can affect the nervous system and create ongoing low-level anxiety and residual fear, which can cause your mind to fabricate a threat that does not exist and distrust when there is no need.

The fear that people have of each other can prevent the taking of intelligent risks in getting to know other people.

Fear feeds judgement, it fosters distrust and isolation and distracts from creativity.

Fear can create conflict between what you want and what you actually do. Between what your mind desires and how your body behaves, between your ego, and your ability to succeed.

An unhealthy ego promotes separation and opposes unity. A healthy ego aids you in becoming resilient.

Fear has a subtle but pervasive way to keep you small, keep you safe, control your life and protect you from activities you would otherwise like to try, from places you would travel to, and good people you might meet.

The small voice of fear continually talks you out of committing yourself to your success.

As a tool of the ego, a fearful mind can dictate the terms of your life.

You know that fear has shown up when you keep putting off an important task or when you avoid a phone call that might bring work because you believe you do not have the right skills, even though you are more than qualified.

Become aware of your fears, see them as a way of keeping you in the comfort and safety of what you have always known and doing what you have always done.

What you resist persists, what you fight against, fights back. If you spend your life afraid of trying new things, your life will be limited. If you do not make decisions about your future life and take action to make it happen, the fear of what you do not know will hold you back

Are you ready to challenge your fears?

Do not' let fear stop you. Embrace your fear. Learn from it. Let it show you what you need so that you can prepare for success.

Spot how you stop yourself from taking action and strengthen your commitment to seeing your projects through to completion.

Is it time to recognize the subconscious tricks that hinder your progress?

Would you put fear in charge of your life, or would you choose the most expansive, open, and resourceful part of you to help create it?

The more you step up to take charge of your life by committing to positive action, fear caused by inaction begins to release its grip. You can then say 'yes' to new experiences.

Are you ready to step out of your own way?

What are your greatest fears

What fears stop you taking action to fulfill your dreams?

What would it take for you to actually create a life of greater possibilities rather than limited by fear?

What would you have to do right now to get started?

TAKE ACTION

Remind yourself every day to choose the life you would live. Be everyday who you would be. Live as though this day be your last precious moment to appreciate all that life has to offer.

Try the following practices to help you overcome your fear:-

- Be aware of thoughts and feelings that pervade your mind and body everyday
- Recognize your projections
- Ask the right questions
- Notice when your decisions are based on fear rather than what you truly desire
- Recognize when you are not being authentic or true to your own heart
- Be open to change
- Be open to other people
- Accept the strength in vulnerability

- Spread positive influence

- Strive for peace instead of retaliation

- It is not your job to fix anybody

- Identify the games you play

- Know when to say, "Enough is Enough"

Taking action is more important than belief in whether or not you can succeed. Uncertainty may persist but action propels you towards success.

CHOOSE HAPPY

Despite our personal levels of sensitivity, and ability to express emotions, we all feel emotions. If you do not experience emotions, there is a dysfunction that needs to be addressed.

As human beings, we share a collective pool of emotions, thoughts, and feelings; we also have basic physical and spiritual needs in common. For example, the human body needs certain nutrients to survive. We need clean air and pure drinking water. This is true for everyone. No matter how dissimilar, in time we all come to experience emotions such as joy or grief.

When our basic needs for shelter, nourishment, rest, renewal, play and the most satisfying of all, love, are satisfied, we have the freedom to fulfil our greatest dreams. You can .choose how to approach each day.

When heartbroken or lonely, or when you judge yourself for expressing tormented feelings, remember that the world's greatest teachers and leaders experienced immense suffering, yet lived through pain to offer solace to others. Are most of your memories happy or sad?

If your memories cause despair, does it make sense to nurture them?

Try the following ideas to start ridding yourself of the pain brought on by memories you would prefer to forget:-

- First acknowledge them
- Observe objectively
- Do not continue to recreate painful memories by reflecting on them
- Do not allow painful memories free rein,

Challenge the memory and its right to still be in your mind

- Listen to joyful music, and inspiring speakers
- Watch comedy and nature programs
- Read biographies
- Inspire others

If your awareness and ability to think clearly are compromised, you can fall into an addictive pattern of doing the same thing and making the same 'mistakes' time and time again.

Can you afford to allow someone else to be in control of your happiness?

You can start the day grumbling or speak words that enliven and lift your spirit.

235

Give yourself a reason to 'take action' rather than be in 'reaction'. Look for joy and possibility rather than remain at the whim of feelings that rise to the surface.

Think of your feelings as personal signposts to self-awareness.

You cannot control everything that life throws at you. Life will happen and things will go wrong, but you can choose to smile as even a half smile can help to lift you up. Choose to brighten someone's day, you might also choose to pay a good deed forward.

Recognizing your predominant mood offers insight into your personality and how you navigate the world. The following question seeks to explore your lingering emotional states, for example is your current personality mostly calm and curious or if you live and conduct your life with underlying tension, aggression, or anger.

Reflect on your daily experiences. What mood do you find yourself in most frequently?

(fill in your own favorite mood)

SELF REFLECTION

What new skills do you now have
and what new awareness have you
received?

Don't worry

everything is gonna be all
right because everything
changes with time.

Take a breath, reflect and
make a choice.

Choose to be happy

Section Seven

MISTRESS OF CREATION

Is it time to create the life you would live if you knew you could live the life you chose?

This section is about stepping deeper into your life to look at where you invest your energy, how to improve relationships, and more.

Your life is not an accident so do not treat it as such.

Many people believe that money is the issue that hinders success. Whilst money is important it is not the main obstacle to getting started.

With focus, commitment and dedication successful entrepreneurs, athletes, musicians, chess players and others rose from absolute poverty to the top of their profession. Money is not the main issue. It is possible to create your dream life.

Be bold in your choices and take steps to create your life. Paint it in beautiful colors by embracing what is different about you. Bring your sense of style to what you do. Start by dressing in ways that make you feel gorgeous. Add touches to your home that make it a place of refuge, safety, and comfort.

The present is all that truly exists. What if you took a leap into the unknown and said 'Yes' to something new?

If anyone tells you that success and riches are quick and easy, they are lying to you. Success does not come without some degree of struggle and sacrifice. There is good reason for the struggle, as the journey itself shapes your thinking and prepares your success.

Your development is the most important part of your success story. Ask any champion what it took for them to make it.

Small steps can lead to big results.

Success cannot come without change, dedication, and commitment. The bigger your steps, the more profound the change, and the faster you grow.

What would it take for this moment to be the beginning of something amazing?

Take one step

You may have good reasons to delay your plans. However, initiating at least one action can bring you closer to living a fuller life. Zero plus zero equals zero. Doing nothing leads zero change.

If you believed yourself the mistress, the author, and the creator of your world, describe the changes you would see in your life.

MANY ARCHETYPES OF WOMAN

You are many things and many archetypes of woman. The word archetype has origins in ancient Greece and means a typical representation or type.

Stereotypes can be harmful, oversimplified, negative and racist depictions of people but archetypes are universally accepted models of human behaviors and character.

Can you find yourself in any of the following?

- Is there a passionate woman that feels deeply, whose strong emotions are sometimes overwhelming?
- Is there a mother that protects others from hurt?
- What about the little girl who sometimes throws tantrums when she

does not get what she wants but who can also be easily pleased?

- Do you recognize the rebellious teenager striding out into the world to discover new experiences?

- Can you appreciate the young woman in love?

Regardless of your age, these women are still inside you. Be aware of which you let direct your life.

Both the 'good' and the 'bad' serve a positive function

It is unlikely that you will be unaffected by other people throughout your life, or that you will not affect others.

Sometime people may play games or try to manipulate you rather than ask for what they want. Accept that human beings, including you, are fallible. No one is perfect. Every human being has strengths and vulnerabilities. You can learn from both.

What you perceive as 'bad' things do happen to 'good' people, but that does not necessarily make you bad. If you are unemployed, facing foreclosure, debt collectors, or carrying deep emotional scars, remember that you are not a victim. You can turn it around.

Conversely good things happen for 'bad' people, but that does not necessarily make them good. The truth is that we all have potential for good and bad, it is our actions that determine the integrity of our choices.

Make a start in unchaining yourself from victimhood:-

- Recognize that you might only be a few steps away from success.

- Become aware of your thoughts

- Recite daily positive affirmations

- Change your perception about yourself.

- Ask for help

- Develop daily practices that remind you of your brilliance

- Make empowering choices

- Know what helps you to feel fully alive

- Show up for yourself.

Do not live by default. if you do not speak up, if you do not make a move, if you do not stand up for yourself, you are disempowering yourself.

if someone's perceptions of you are flawed, if they look for the worst in you rather than seeing the best, if they accuse you of what they in actuality exhibit, then do not define yourself based on their point of view.

Be willing to hear uncomfortable information, listen to perspectives that help you to fly, and most of all do not limit yourself before you have begun.

How would YOU describe you?

Section Seven - Invest your energy wisely

Trying to change other people is a waste of time and energy, instead, invest in yourself.

Make a list of projects that you previously put aside, into which you could now invest your time?

ALLOW LIFE TO FLOW

Give yourself permission to change and make room for clearer ideas and better circumstances to appear.

Your life is only wasted if YOU waste it

Let things that are outside your control be what they will be. Decide carefully which battles are worth fighting and those to leave alone. All things in life work to show you a direction that you could take to a better life, Notice the signs.

There is a difference between what feels genuine and good to your mind, body, and spirit, and what does not.

Your difficulties provide valuable information about your potential for greatness, but potential is nothing without action to support it.

253

The deeper you dig into your reserves of emotional strength to pull yourself out of a situation, the more wisdom and experience you will be able to offer.

Do not give up on developing yourself. Learn new skills, meet new people, remember your dreams, work through your moods, be brave in your decision-making, and keep going.

Allow life to flow to you, then through you to other people

Take one day at a time, one step at a time to plan your future.

You can make it.

SEX AND THE SINGLE GIRL

An enjoyable sex life is a fun way to create deeper connection between two people. It promotes greater intimacy, helps maintain a unique bond, and contributes to a fulfilling relationship. After all sexual activity brought us into being, and keeps the earth populated.

Although sex can be an exquisite experience for some, that is not true for everyone. For some people sex is problematic.

The desire for sex can be affected by emotions, hormone levels, tiredness, desire, attraction, fear, stress, physiology, religious beliefs, upbringing they all play a role.

If sex is difficult for you or causes distress, speak with your physician or other practitioner to help you find a solution.

Desire, touch, and intimacy trigger chemical reactions in the body that might be interpreted or misinterpreted as love and lead to emotional hurt when it is discovered otherwise.

Some people use the idea of relationship in order to get sex. Some believe that sex is the beginning of a relationship whilst the other person sees it as just one night of fun. Become aware of the difference in your expectations.

Sex alone without appreciation, compassion, gratitude, and communication, will not lead to a relationship that matures and becomes more meaningful over time.

Use the following questions to help you reflect on the potential future of any enjoyable night.

- What type of future do either of you want?

- Are either of you looking for more beyond these moments of pleasure?

- If you choose to continue into a relationship, what do you know about this person and would you make compatible partners?

- Do you have similar ideas about what a relationship means?

- Are you trying to make an ill-matched relationship work?

Answer the questions on the following pages, going into detail about the type of relationship you would like to cultivate.

Describe your ideal relationship

What qualities and values are most
important to you in a partner?

What behavior can you absolutely not abide or live with?

What qualities do You bring to a relationship?

Be courageous in
choosing what generates
greater possibilities

LOVE COURAGEOUSLY

Love as an energy exists independently. To move through people, it requires a relay, a channel and someone ready to receive. The relay is the person ready to send love. The channel is communication between two people, whether in speech, deed, or touch, and of course someone who is open to being loved.

Love is energy freely available to anyone who chooses to receive

In things of the heart there is no guarantee that your love will be returned but to know love, you have to take the risk of being open to receive it.

Have you heard the saying "love is a choice"?

There are times that you may not like your family but in order to nurture, develop and maintain those relationships, you choose to continue loving them, despite your upset or hurt feelings.

Recognize when to let go but never give up on your dreams of a better life!

Have you tried molding a troubled relationship into a vision of what you want it to be, yet despite your best efforts, it will not fit? Do not live in a fantasy world, recognize your current reality, and change it. The "ride or die" relationship can be destructive.

In a toxic relationship your best choice is to love yourself by walking away. If you do not have clarity, take a beat, ease back, stop talking, and observe.

The information you need might be right in front of you

True love is not wishy washy

Until someone decides that change is a good thing for them, accept that the behavior you see in front of you is what you will continue to get, Things are as they are.

Be calm and consider what your inner awareness tells you about your next best steps. What will it take for you to find peace of mind?

In the middle of your turmoil you may not see it, but as one door closes, others will open. You do have other options.

When betrayed by a lover or let down by a friend it is hard to remember that you are loved and there are people out there who would genuinely appreciate you when you are willing to open your heart and let them in. Perhaps you cannot see them right now because you are full of residual emotions from your previous relationship, but there are many loving people alive in the world.

Loving another may sometimes hurt, but true love does not seek to hurt or harm you.

Do not overlook abuse. Do not overlook unkind and unjust behavior. Most of all do not overlook a lack of empathy and compassion.

Do not harden yourself against hurt, soften to love.

Love is more than material gifts received, more than just a word. Love is seen and felt in a person's words and actions. Some actions build trust, other conduct most definitely drives love away.

When considering your current relationship or looking for a loving connection, start by observing yourself.

Do you behave in any of the following ways?

- Is your first instinct to reject when intimacy is what you really want?

- Are you shouting and pushing away when what you want is to be held?

- Are you the first to attack to ensure you are on top?

The entire world could use a lesson in love, so role model what you would like to receive. In the meantime, here are a set of behaviors that demonstrate love and allow it to flourish.

- Appreciation

- Vulnerability

- Gratitude

- Intimacy

- Communication

- Connection

A successful, nurturing relationship comes from a willingness to be vulnerable and intimate. It means choosing to let go of resentment and always seek ways to communicate.

The challenges of relationships and family life give you an opportunity to learn and to grow. Demonstrate in words and actions that you value the people in your life.

Gratitude and obvious appreciation for those with whom you share your life, helps relationships to flourish and create a future with even greater possibilities and deeper connection. When upset with your loved ones refer to the Loving Toolkit below and on page 271.to assist you in creating peace.

Loving Toolkit No. 1 Ask yourself the following questions:
How would you genuinely want that argument to end?
Is it safe for you to be vulnerable? If it is not safe, you should not be there.
How might you reach out to your loved one?
Be open, vulnerable, and willing to speak from your heart. Is the transgression forgivable?
Are you willing to forgive?
What do you really want for this moment?

Rather than escalate an argument, give yourself a moment to let the spark dissipate. Breathe deeply to oxygenate your lungs and clear your mind. Take a walk and whilst doing that, practice forgiveness. You cannot maintain a great relationship without learning to forgive.

Although it might be of help to face each other, that is not always necessary and could lead to more upset. A genuine forgiveness practice takes place in your mind and your body first.

Depending on circumstances and personalities you may need this practice daily.

First forgive yourself, then in your mind forgive the other person. Do not say the words "I forgive you" as it could sound patronizing, but an apology when necessary and demonstration of love is important.

The practice of forgiveness is for your own benefit, and for the benefit of the relationship as the relationship itself has its own character and identity. There is you, the other person, then the two of you together.

The two of you can survive without each other but the relationship cannot.

If parents did not love and forgive their children, they might leave them by the roadside. If children did not love and forgive their parents, they might never speak to them again.

No matter how hard it may feel to try practicing forgiveness, if you have a good relationship, it will be worth your time.

Too often a previous 'bad' experience can skew the perception of a current relationship causing either person to shut down or shut out, in order not to get hurt.

Maintaining a loving relationship takes time, attention, and effort. At the heart of a great relationship is the willingness to remain open to each other despite your differences, It requires allowance for your partner to be themself and not expecting them to be you. Do you want to be right all the time, or do you want to remain happy and together?

Do not sweat the small stuff

Be aware of when you are unwilling to let go of being right. If your partner does not wash dishes in the way that you do, then get a dishwasher. Are you willing to ruin a great relationship over something small?

Loving Toolkit No. 2 Keep the following ideas in mind:-
• *Good times take care of themselves, challenging times, let you know what needs your attention*
• *Actively plan your good times in order to offset the bad*
• *Open your eyes and be willing to see the reality of the relationship you are in, rather than a fairytale idea in your head that only you want.*
• *If the relationship is not right for you, knowing the truth will set you free*
• *Stay open to your person*
• *Rather than choosing to be 'right', choose what is best for the relationship*

Loving Toolkit No. 2
Keep the following ideas in mind:-

- *Be willing to recognize when they get it wrong and love them anyway.*

- *Do not expect the other person to be perfect, see them for who they are right now with their own history, challenges, and struggles. Find your compassion and empathy*

- *Is this the type of person with whom you would choose to spend more of your precious time?*

- *Would the relationship work if you were both stranded on a dessert island? would you be happy in their company?*

- *What is the quality of your communication?*

Answer the following: questions:-

What is the nature and quality of your current intimate relationship?

What was the nature of your previous intimate relationship?

What is the current nature of your family relationships?

How well do you relate to other people in general?

What would improve all your relationships?

Love, like all else in life, is a choice. Implicit in that choice are a set of behaviors that allow love to flourish

Appreciation, Vulnerability, Gratitude, Intimacy, Communication, and Connection

SELF-CARE

When dishing out care and kisses, remember to add yourself to the list. Do not wait for someone to love or care for you before you start caring for yourself.

Life is short and the years go by quicker than you think so go ahead and show yourself some love...!

Buy yourself flowers, take yourself on vacation, get a massage because the more you love yourself, the more others will learn how to love you.

In place of carrying your troubles around as if attached to your back, make it a priority to find something joyful about every day.

Decide to bring laughter and inspiration into each environment that you find yourself, do not force it on others, just let it radiate from you.

As you channel love and spread it around, it will find its way back to you through others.

Remember that love is shown by appreciation, vulnerability, gratitude, intimacy, communication, and connection. Describe below what you do to show your body how much you appreciate it for taking care of you?

BE GRATEFUL FOR LIFE'S BLESSINGS

Gratitude alters the brain's chemistry and affirms life. Gratitude is not a way of living in denial and ignoring the reality of what goes on around you. Neither is it a reason to diminish other people's reality. [3]

Gratitude allows you to learn something new from every situation by asking 'what' and 'how' rather than 'why.'

- 'What can this situation teach me about myself?'

- 'What is the worst thing that could happen?'

- 'What do I want to happen next?'

- 'What else is possible?'

- 'How best can I use this situation?'

---

[3] See:- *The Gratitude Journal*, page 311

With gratitude your trials offer an opportunity to recognize the influences that keep you in pain. It can be a tool in changing old addictive habits and replacing them with beneficial behaviors.

Gratitude gives you a reason to smile, and if there is one thing that can enhance your beauty far more than makeup and better than designer clothing, it is a smile.

Make a note below of the ways in which your life could change if you made an ever-renewing choice to be gracious about life and grateful for life's blessings.

Make a note below of what you
could choose to be grateful for at this time.

Wear a smile.

It is your best feature, and

costs nothing.

It elevates the mood of

everyone around and

attracts positive people

CHANGE AND TRANSITION

Human Beings love comfort and routine because rituals and habits make us feel safe. Comfort allows our bodies to find rest and renewal.

Even the most adventurous wanderer at some point, seeks comfort and a return to routine before venturing off again.

Change and transition are an important and natural part of life and occur throughout life. Too much comfort leads to inertia, too much activity or struggle can lead to stress and ill health.

Change is important in different areas of life. Getting too comfortable in a relationship can lead to taking the other person for granted and not appreciating the part they play in your life. Getting too comfortable in a mundane job leads to apathy and resignation to an environment you do not like.

Nature, which also includes human beings, uses cycles, patterns, and transition from one season to the next to maintain order and the survival of each species.

Transition, change, habituation, and transformation are an inevitable part of the natural cycle. The seasons, tides, phases of the moon, the flowering of bulbs, animal migration, night, and day, recurrently change and demonstrate habituation.

Habituation is when we fall into sync with the environment around us.

The British researcher, biologist and quantum physicist Rupert Sheldrake coined the term Morphic Fields and Morphic Resonance to help explain how plants grow from spores or seeds into the characteristics of their species, for example how the leaf of a specific tree adopts the same shape as other leaves of that genus.

What Sheldrake and other scientists found was that all species have an invisible template within, and surrounding the body that contains a blueprint of what they are and what they grow into. You could call it an inbuilt memory from previous generations.

Change your environment, alter your DNA, change your life

New generations contribute to the template, thereby adding their own patterns to future generations, inherited through Morphic Resonance. This is how we come to resemble our family.

What these findings mean to us as humans is that every single cell in the human body contains all the information that it needs to grow.

Nevertheless, we can deliberately alter the template by changing environment whether physically or psychologically. We can change physically by migrating or psychologically via what we eat and what we do to our bodies.

You do not have to become your parent... Become the YOU... that You choose to be.

Although the change of environment might mean a physical relocation, you do not have to move. According to Sheldrake, you can change your personal space by cleaning and decluttering your home, having beautiful things in and around your home, by the kind of pictures you hang on the wall, the quality of the textiles you use, for example natural fabric such as cotton has a better effect on the body than synthetic material such as polyester because everything carries a vibrational resonance that has a subtle effect on you.

You can change your internal environment with exercise, food, and awareness of the music, movies, and books you consume, as well as the people with whom you associate every day.

It is said that we become the people with whom we spend most of our time so what does your environment, your friends, and the foods you eat say about the future you are creating?

Describe below some of the changes you could make to what you eat, to your grooming, with the type of people with

whom you associate, with your job,
and how you live.

	What will you change
Food	
Grooming	
People	
Work	
Home	
Other	

In the space below say more about the changes you will make.

Change does not happen

without first becoming

aware of the need to

change

SELF REFLECTION

What new skills do you now have and
what new awareness have you
received?

Be yourself ...
Shine your
brightest!

Life is art!

can you see the funny

side?

(or at least discover what makes you smile)

Engage laughter,

spread humour, bring

joy. ....It works!

Section Eight

REFLECT AND REVIEW

Today's Date_____

The reason you started this journey may have shifted. Now is a suitable time to reflect on what you have achieved so far this year and consider new measures of success because as you grow, as your projects evolve, everything changes.

You are now in an ongoing cycle of creative endeavor that requires you to check in regularly and assess if you are still on course or need to shift where you are heading.

YOUR MOST RECENT SUCCESS

What have you accomplished so far this year?

What did you learn this year?

What remains outstanding on your to-do list?

NEW MEASURES OF SUCCESS

Look back to page 28 where you described what success meant to you. Describe what success means to you now and how it might have changed.

What is your new plan of action?

LOOK AHEAD TO THE NEXT 5 YEARS

What would you like to do during the next five years?

Year One

Year Two

Year Three

Year Four

Year Five

You committed your time to this journey and are on the road to discovering even more about what are capable of achieving. and creating.

You can look forward to more remarkable years of success.

Section Nine

BOOKS

This book belongs to a series designed specifically to assist women in living authentically empowered lives. Gift this book to a friend Or try one of the titles below.

Shaping Your Life from the Inside Out Workbook	Provides a systematic approach to transforming your life with self-affirming and practical exercises to create lasting change.
Plan Your Most Successful Year Ever	The personal success planner that guides you step-by-step to refining your goals, monitoring your progress, and realizing your dreams.
Planner Companion	Additional pages for creating lists, writing your reflections, and journaling your progress.
The Gratitude Journal	Shifting your perspective from victim of circumstance to mistress of creation.
This Day I Call Your Name	Book of prayers, poetic words of inspiration, encouragement to lift your spirit, & brighten your day.
Looking Ahead to the Next 5 Years	Assists you to plan the future where you live how you choose, rather than by circumstances alone.

ONLINE PROGRAMS & COURSES

Create a Year of Success	This course will teach you: how to recognize the knowledge, wisdom, and experience that you have gathered over the years, and how to use those life experiences to bolster your success.
Time2Shine Consultation Program	In this 6-week program you will create a plan of action to get you to your goals faster. You have several private virtual meetings with me, plus follow up emails. We look at your most pressing concerns, how to eliminate them, then prioritize your next steps.

AUDIO

Taking a Bird's Eye View	Guided visualization audio for stress relief and visualizing your goals
1 (One) Minute Wonder podcast	A 1-to-3-minute podcast to rewire your brain to create a new reality. Listen on Spotify

WEBSITE

www.createayearofsuccess.com

Are you having fun yet?

What else is

possible?